Reflections |

Poetry and Affirmations for Those
Seeking Purpose and Peace

By R. Wright

Don't ask
permission
to be Yourself.
@THEWRIGHTLETTERS

You really are unique.
You ARE special.
You're one of a kind.
So don't hesitate one second
to be that YOU.
Don't ask permission to
be your authentic, true self.
What will that feel like?
You'll know because you
won't be hiding.
You won't feel shame.
You won't be pretending.
You'll feel peace.
You'll be able to stop trying
to be somebody you're not.
You'll feel at home.
At home in your own body.
At home in your own soul.
And finally at home in your mind.

USE YOUR
fear
DON'T BE SWALLOWED UP BY IT.
@THEWRIGHTLETTERS

When you feel afraid
know that you are
in the company
of all who come before
and after.
Fear itself doesn't
have to be scary.
It's the common
denominator that makes
us more alike than different.
Your response to the fear is what matters.
It's your response to the fear that
can change the trajectory of your life.
Acknowledge it and use it,
but don't be swallowed up
or paralyzed by it.

RELeASe
-the-
BURDeN
-of-
EXPeCTaTioN.

@THEWRIGHTLETTERS

If you find yourself
trying to measure up
against real and imaginary peers,
trying to meet some impossible
standard of perfection,
or trying hard to live how you're expected to,
stop and change course.
Release the burden of expectations
you're carrying.
And begin doing what you were meant to.
Spend your life living authentically.
Not comparing, not striving; simply being.
Living fully and living joyfully.
Free yourself from the pressure
you were never intended to feel.

feel it all
AND THEN MOVE THROUGH IT.

Let me share a secret.
Your feelings are not wrong.
They're messengers.
Letting you know you're alive.
They're barometers measuring
your response to an experience.
Try not to ignore them.
Don't push them away.
Instead, feel your feelings.
Treat them kindly.
And then what happens next
is what makes all the difference.
That's right.
Feel it all.
And then, move through it.
Move through to acceptance.
Move through to peace.
And then do it all again.

I hope you see yourself as I do.
@THEWRIGHTLETTERS

How do you see yourself
in a world that asks us to
be more, do more?
I hope it is as I see you.
Full of goodness.
Full of mystery.
Full of grace.
Full of energy.
Full of love.
Full of possibility.
In a world that wants you to be just enough,
but not too much.
I hope you see yourself as you are.
Just as you were made to be.
Save the energy spent continually striving.
And instead spend it living.
One big, beautiful--sometimes complicated--life.
Live it with eyes that see yourself clearly.
Gently.
Kindly.
Fully.
And always truthfully.

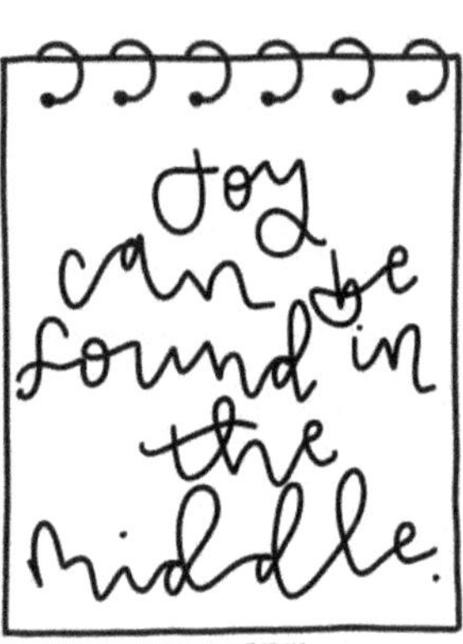
Joy
can be
found in
the
middle.
@THEWRIGHTLETTERS

Do you notice we're often told joy can only be found in the highs?

Real happiness only comes at the top of the mountain?

True contentment can only be felt when you have finally arrived?

But joy can actually be found in the middle too.

The mundane is full of moments we shouldn't be so quick to dismiss.

There are many of these moments.

Be sure to catch them when they come.

Much of our lives is spent not at the top or the bottom, but in that middle.

The in between.

And when we stop, the beauty, the gratitude, the awe can all be felt there too.

So don't be saddened that the climb seems too hard and that wholeness seems to never come.

You can claim peace, joy, "okayness" right where you are.

It's available.

It's freeing.

It's yours.

PAY ATTENTION TO WHAT

lights

YOU UP.

@THEWRIGHTLETTERS

What lights you up?
Is there something you do that makes time stand
still?
Something that, while you're doing it, makes you
feel more YOU?
Do more of this.
It doesn't have to make sense to others.
Sometimes it might not even make sense to you.
But what it brings you, the feeling of
contentment it offers, will.
Finding your purpose might feel elusive, but
it will be worth the quest.
You have permission to do what you were
created to do
whether others get it or not.
Whether they understand your pursuits is of no
concern to you.
So be open to what brings you that spark of joy.
Your purpose will find you.
And this will bring you peace.

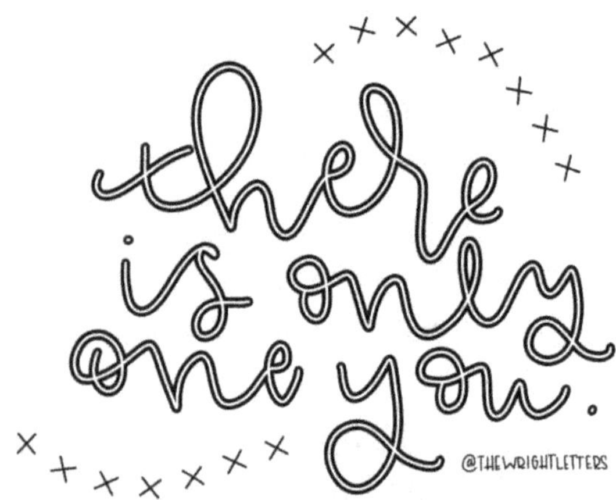

there is only one you.
@THEWRIGHTLETTERS

There is only one you.
I know, you've been told this your whole life.
Or maybe you have not.
But it's true.
And it means only you can offer this world what you can offer it.
When it doesn't feel this simple,
When it doesn't feel like you have any unique qualities.
When it feels, in fact, like you're an imposter.
Just imitating those around you.
Or pretending to be what everyone expects.
Remember this truth.
There is only one you.
Nobody else is you.
Nobody else has lived your life.
Nobody else has your story.
Own that. Believe it. Be proud of it.

THE ACT OF
hope
IS POWERFUL.
@THEWRIGHTLETTERS

On those days
when you feel despair
or just not quite like yourself,
when you're not sure you can keep
feeling the way you are,
don't lose hope.
Hope that it can be different.
Hope that it will get better.
And hope that you will once
again feel like you.
Believe it to be true.
The act of hope is powerful.
So cling to the possibility
that this is just a moment.
And that another one, a better one,
is on its way to you.

SHARE YOUR

STORY.

@THEWRIGHTLETTERS

Share your story
with those who have earned the right to hear it.
And with those who feel safe.
With those who support
and want the best for you.
Knowing that your pain, your struggle, your
difficulties
might speak to them.
And your achievements, victories, and happiness
will be a cause of celebration for them as well.
Give your story room to be heard and felt.
And in doing so become heard and known
by those who matter most in your life.

DON'T LET A

limited

VIEW STEAL YOUR JOY.

Don't let a limited view steal your joy.
If only we could see ourselves, our situations,
our lives
with perspective, a fuller scope, a wider lens.
We would see how capable we are,
how much beauty there is
even in the pain.
We might be able to walk through life
a little more joyful.
A little more satisfied.
A little more grateful.
When you feel inadequate, uncertain, and as if
you'll never arrive,
Stop and notice the good.
Don't dismiss the bad.
You won't be able to blind yourself to it entirely.
But widen your lens enough to see a bigger
picture.
It's always there.

KEEP
SHINING
bright.

Keep shining bright.
Don't dim your light.
When the world tries to make you smaller,
resist the urge to give in.
Spread your essence.
Share your joy.
Be you in all your glory.
The ones who see your glow
will warm themselves in it,
will catch your flame and shine too.
So keep your shine
And stay true to you.
It is all you're asked to do.
It is all you're all asked to be.

BE
present.
@THEWRIGHTLETTERS

Remain present.
It's one of the hardest things to do.
We're so inclined to look back or look ahead.
But the not-so-simple act of staying in the
present moment
is the act that will bring you the most happiness.
The most fulfillment.
Remove all distractions.
At least for a little while.
Set aside time to fully embrace the life you are
living.
Experience it with awareness.
Be present.
Even when you're tempted by what's
pulling you from all sides.
Your reward will be a contentment and
satisfaction
that only comes by giving yourself wholly
to the present moment.

HOLD
SPACE
FOR
OTHERS.

Hold space for others.
Be there for them
when they need you.
Listen.
Learn.
They don't always need a fix,
sometimes just a listening ear,
a shoulder to cry on,
or simply an understanding heart will do.
Let them feel and share.
Be a safe place for them to land.

TIME SPENT ON
YOU
IS ALWAYS WORTH IT.
@THEWRIGHTLETTERS

Time spent on you is not time wasted.
You are worth it.
You are worth the minutes.
The stolen moments.
The self work you do will pay off in dividends.
You are your best investment.
Put aside the guilt
and the pressure to invest only in others.
It is when you realize your own worth that
you will begin to see others' true value.
And the love you pour into yourself
will overflow onto those around you.

comparison robs you
of your chance at
contentment.

It's so easy to fall into the trap of comparison.
What's more difficult is to stop and remember
you don't know their story.
Their journey.
Nobody began in the same place.
Nobody walks the same road.
Try to stay on your own path.
Find joy in your own experiences.
Enjoy that feeling of contentment.
Instead of giving into the temptation of
comparing your situation to those around you,
don't miss the good in your own story.
And rest knowing
it is the only one you are meant to write.

LIVE FROM A PLACE OF
abundance.

@THEWRIGHTLETTERS

There is so much good to go around.
You'll find greater peace if you strive to
live from a place of abundance.
Believe there is no shortage.
Say no to a scarcity mentality.
When the world tells you to
compete, cheat, and take what is yours,
Rest knowing there is enough for all.
Live in abundance.
Spread abundance.
Share in the abundance.
Do it guilt free as you begin to grasp
what was always meant for you.

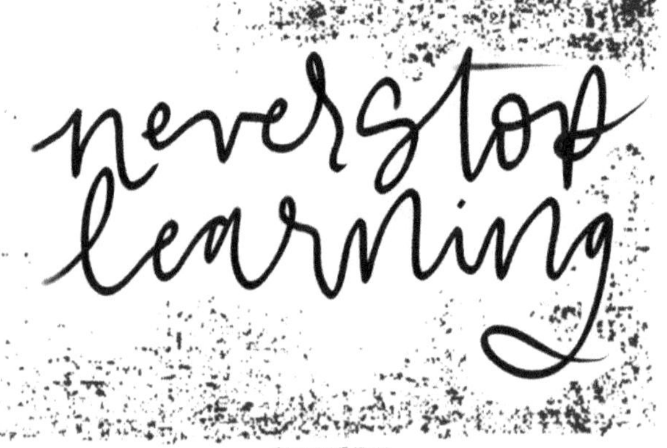
never stop
learning
@THEWRIGHTLETTERS

Embrace the lifelong learner inside of you.
Keep thirsting for more.
Fill yourself with knowledge.
But also strive to gain perspective, inspiration.
When we are open to others' stories,
our minds and hearts become more open too.
The way you learn and what you devote
yourself to
might look different from that of others.
That's okay.
That's good.
That makes you you.
Seek out what your heart is intent on finding,
knowing, receiving.
Just never stop learning.
Your life will be richer.
And your love will be fuller.

practice
GRATITUDE
@THEWRIGHTLETTERS

Live a life of gratitude, they say.
Sometimes it comes easy.
Sometimes it takes a little work.
But each time you're intentional
about practicing gratitude
you'll be surprised
at your mind shift.
Your heart shift.
In a complicated world
stopping to notice that you still have
so much to be thankful for
can be the balm to your soul
you didn't know you needed.
Start small. Or big.
Speak it.
Write it.
Or just feel it.
Accept the power a shift towards gratitude
can have
in your also messy, but oh so beautiful, life.

find the good.
@THEWRIGHTLETTERS

Find the good.
It's all around.
Eyes wide open.
Search for it.
Don't miss it.
Life isn't always beautiful.
It's confusing. Complicated.
But also magical.
And alongside the bad
is a lot of good.
Notice it.
It will save you.

PROTECT YOUR

peace.

It might cost you those who don't understand,
but I hope you know
the great value in
protecting your peace.
You are not required to engage in
toxic, unhealthy interactions or
remain in damaging relationships.
You are allowed to say no.
Your body and spirit even require it.
So protect your peace.
Protect your calm.
Protect your heart and your mind.
Choose life-giving relationships.
You are worth it.

take
time to
grieve.

@THEWRIGHTLETTERS

Grieve freely.
There will be hurt in life.
There will be loss.
You'll have to let go of people, ideas, and
experiences
you thought you would have.
Feel all you need to feel.
Take your time.
Others might try to tell you
how to grieve and limit the
expanse of your emotions.
Grieve guilt free.
Accept that grief is a sacred experience.
Trust yourself.
Trust the process,
knowing it looks different
for everybody.
And never give up hope as you say goodbye
to what is no longer yours in the way that it once
was.

it's okay to say

NO.

It's okay to say no.
It's even good.
A lot is continually asked of you.
You feel pulled and pushed and
burdened by expectations.
Begin the ultimate act of
self love by doing what it takes to
prioritize you.
Reject what is not meant for you.
Say no when you need to.
Make caring for yourself a priority
so that love can build up and pour out.
So you can find peace and contentment.
Without a trace of guilt.

LET YOUR
MOTIVATION
COME FROM
within.
@THEWRIGHTLETTERS

Let your motivation come from within.
If you find yourself seeking outside motivation
or affirmation from others
and notice you're continually falling short
or feeling like a failure,
know that it's okay.
You'll never be able to stay motivated if working
for the approval of others.
And you'll likely never receive exactly the
affirmation you need.
Instead, turn inward.
What you need is right there.
Root for you.
Cheer for you.
Encourage yourself on.
And when you stick with your goal,
finally reaching it or simply knowing you gave it
your all,
YOU will be proud of you and that
will be enough.

Something
better
is on the
horizon
@THEWORDSOFLETTERS

Something better is on the horizon.
Endings can be hard.
They can feel like a loss.
But sometimes they can be
the start of something new.
Something good.
Something even better.
Grieve the end, but
keep hope that
Something better is on its way.
There is more good coming than
you can even imagine.

Don't
stop
evolving.
@THEWRIGHTLETTERS

Don't stop evolving.
It is inevitable. You will change.
Change really is the only constant.
But don't worry.
It is a good thing.
You will grow.
You will learn.
You will experience more and more.
And soon, you'll have evolved
and might even surprise yourself
with the new gentleness with which
you now view the world and others.
You might surprise others
with a version of you they didn't expect.
Don't let that deter you
from becoming exactly who
you are meant to be.

you
are beautiful
on the
inside too .
@THEWRIGHTLETTERS

You are beautiful on the inside too.
In this world we live in,
one that places importance on image
and a high priority on beauty, know that
it's your inner spirit that shines through the
brightest.
You are beautiful.
And whole.
This might be evident on the outside.
But your inner beauty is what lasts.
It is what stays with people after they meet you,
spend time with you, and really know you.
It is what makes you truly you.
And it is what matters the most.
So don't forget
you are beautiful on the inside too.

just because you're not there yet, doesn't mean you never will be.
@THEROUGHLETTERS

You will get there.
Practice saying not yet.
You haven't completed that...yet.
You haven't made it...yet.
You haven't reached that goal...yet.
There's so much power in the word yet.
Just because you're not there yet,
doesn't mean you never will be.
Keep a growth mindset.
Don't give up.
And whatever you do,
believe you will reach what you're reaching for
some day.
Maybe not today. Maybe not yet.
But one day,
you will get there.
As you knew deep down all along that you would.

you have value not
because of what you
can do or have done,
but simply because of
who you are.

@THEWRIGHTLETTERS

You have value because you're you.
Your value isn't linked to your accomplishments.
You have value not because of what you have
done
or what you can do,
but simply because you exist.
Has anybody told you your worth
doesn't lie in what you are
able to achieve
or do for others?
It's true.
You have inherent value.
Believe that.
Don't downplay it.
Know your worth.
Act accordingly.
The world will be better for it.
And so will you.

SPEND YOUR
LIFE REALLY
living.
@THEWRIGHTLETTERS

Spend your life really living.
This doesn't mean just staying busy,
but rather just soaking up the moments.
Being still. Taking risks. Living in the present.
Even though it feels hard sometimes.
Make time for those you love.
Embrace the time you spend together.
Make it count.
Say no to routine occasionally.
Say yes to spontaneity.
Fill your days making memories.
The Big. Small. Mundane.
Knowing you'll look back feeling as if you
spent your life really living.
Fully living.
A life not wasted.

Take
a
risk.
@THEWRIGHTLETTERS

Take a risk.
once in a while.
Step outside your comfort zone.
Do something even
if you need to do it afraid.
Live on the edge a bit.
Even if it doesn't look scary to others,
it might be the hardest thing you've ever
attempted.
Face it head on.
There's no failure when you try.
Enjoy the ride.
Ride the high.
Take a risk
And feel alive.
Feel brave.
Feel more you.

Reflections |

Write your own affirmations.
Play around with poetry.
Doodle your heart out.
Create your story.
Live it out.